CW00501718

DEAR DAYDREAMS

a collection of poems by
Ash Elizabeth

These words are a reflection
of the way that I so often
feel inside, but rarely give a
voice to. I've given it a
voice now.

To daydreams

Dear Daydreams

It's a bittersweet thought,
But I wonder sometimes:
If I were happy,
Would you leave me?
And if so,
Would it be terrible of me
To miss you?

Dangerously Intimate

Sometimes I don't think I long for a lover
So much as I long for someone
To share the deepest, darkest parts of myself with.
Because doing so
Has always felt
Too dangerously intimate,
Like the space in between
A lit match
And gasoline.

Death of a Star

You are a supernova.
You outshine every galaxy in a brilliant burst of light.
You are the most elegant form of madness I've ever seen,
And there is nothing I would love more
Than to stand small on Earth,
And watch your lights stretch across the cosmos
Until one of us fades forever.

Garden

If a flower grew
With each kiss I planted,
You would be
A garden by now.

Make-Believe

I do wonder sometimes
If love and all its trappings
Are nothing but make-believe.
But then,
I've always loved playing pretend.

If I write a novel,
If I go to London,
If I dye my hair blue
And go after
Everything that I want,
Will that make
Being alone any easier?

Visiting

I wondered what you would think
As you drove through the streets
Of my hometown.
I wanted you to get to know
Every crack in the pavement,
Every bump in the road.
I wanted to know what you thought
As you saw the place where I grew up.
Would you, too, be in awe
Of the house on the corner
With all of the flowers?
Would you smile at the Christmas lights
Still hung up in June?
Would you fall in love
With the uneven sidewalks?
Would you feel the weight
Of all the memories I've made?
I never found out,
Because you never came;
What I had with you faded
Like sidewalk chalk in the rain.

Cartography

I could map out every inch of you,
Draw red lines from freckle to freckle,
Study the planes, the divots,
The topography of your skin,
And still you would be
Unknown territory.
Just like I could study the stars for years,
And still think that they are magic.

Nightmares

Lately I've found
That I fear good dreams
Much more than nightmares.
I wake from a nightmare
And am relieved
That none of it was real.
I wake from a good dream
And hurt
For the same reason.

Thank You

Thank you for kissing me on the cheek.
Thank you for noticing the way I hid behind my bangs.
Thank you for not making me feel bad about it.
Thank you for the flowers.
Thank you so, so much for the flowers.
Thank you for the long messages.
Thank you for the short ones.
Thank you for stopping me halfway down the hall,
Just to bring me in for a hug.
Thank you for the letters, even after all these years.
I've kept them all, you know.

Ink

I could write about you,
Over and over,
Fill up page after page,
Book after book
But still,
All you would ever be is ink.

End Well

We didn't end well,
You and I,
But god
I loved the way we started.

Wish You Were Here

I don't wish you were here,
But thank you
For being there when you were.

3am Thoughts

I want 3am thoughts,
I want secrets in the dark,
I want the poetry you've memorized,
I want the side of you that you try to hide.
I want to meet you on the rooftop
And sit on the gritty tiles and talk.
I want to look at the stars and feel so small,
Then look back at you and forget about it all.

Company

The idea of you keeps me company,
Because a fantasy can't hurt me,
And yet I've never felt a pain so sharp,
Than when I open my eyes
And I'm still alone in the dark.

Know You

I don't think I want to kiss you
As much as I want to know you.

Out of Reach

I only ever seem to love
What is just out of my reach;
Perhaps the beauty of stars
Lies in their distance from us.

Empty Houses

There is a house in your heart
That I don't live in anymore.
I called it home once,
I belonged there; I was sure.

And the house, though still there,
Has no memory of me.
Someone else lives there now.
I'm sure that it's lovely.

There is a house in my heart
That you don't live in anymore.
It was home to you once,
You belonged there; I was sure.

And the house, still there,
Remains full of memories.
The photos hurt to look at,
But the picture frames are lovely.

Please

It's written in all that I do.
In the way that I move,
The way that I speak,
The way that I put up my hair.
It's in the words that I write,
The flowers on my dress,
The blush that I put on my cheeks.
It's written and it says,
Please
Please
Please
Fall in love with me.

To This Day

To this day,
I still think so fondly
Of the way you kissed me:

Like you couldn't help it.

Field of Thorns

Something you must know about me
Is that I hold onto hope for far too long;
I will walk through a field of thorns
For the promise of a rose at the end.

In the Same Breath

My dreams of you
Are so vivid at times
That I can hardly believe
You're not flesh and bone.
I see you,
I hear you,
I feel you like a weight,
But I wake
And you're gone
Because you were never here.
I love you and I lose you
All in the same breath.

Listen

I still listen to that song, you know.
I think of you every time.
I think your voice
Is part of it now.

Always Autumn

I used to imagine us
Sitting at the base of a tree,
Looking out onto an open field.
It was always autumn in this place,
And the sun was always setting
In that perfect way
That bathes everything in gold.
And all we ever did there was talk.

What does it say about me
That at one time my most beloved fantasy
Was to talk with someone I felt connected to
And feel in my bones that I was understood?

And what does it say about me
That the people and places in this fantasy
Have changed over time,
But the core of the fantasy has not?

Daisy

I could take a daisy from the garden
And pick the petals off one by one;
He loves me, he loves me not,
She loves me, she loves me not,
But I think
I'd rather keep the daisy.

Distant Murmur

I hear you like a muffled hum,
A distant murmur
In the quiet hours of the night.
You wake me,
You wake me,
You wake me,
But I don't want
To go back to sleep.

I Want

I want, and I want,
And I ache, and I ache,
For something I can't name.
I want you,
But I don't know who you are.
You're an empty space
That takes the shape
Of a body I can't hold.
You're a ghost in the night,
A mirage in the desert.
You're a ship out on the ocean,
And I am on the shore.
But even if I reached you,
You would disappear.
You were never real.
Still I want, and I want,
And I ache, and I ache,
So even if you're just a ghost,
Hold me with hollow arms,
And tell me everything will be okay.

Cave Paintings

My mind is a cave, and your handprint is there on the wall.
Has been for years and will be for thousands more.

My Name

I don't like my name;
It doesn't belong to me.
I'm a stranger to the sound of it,
It never felt like mine, you see.
So someone, give me a new name,
Call me by anything else:
Darling,
Friend,
Silly girl,
Reshape how I see myself.
Make my name on your lips into something precious,
Carve it into something new.
But whatever you call me,
Dear god,
Make it remind me,
That I belong to myself
As much as to you.

Echo

I call out into the night,
And my echo calls back to me.
It's nice to hear another voice.
We talk for hours, she and I.
But there's something hollow in an echo,
You know?

There's something hollow in me, too,
I think.

A Wildflower Heart

I have a wildflower for a heart;
It grows almost anywhere.
I fall a little bit in love with everyone.
But the thing about wildflowers
Is that they're wild, you know?
They weren't meant to be picked and put in a vase.
I wasn't meant to be on display.
My heart lives at the edge of the woods,
In cracks in the pavement,
In sprawling meadows
And on the side of the highway.
I fall a little bit in love with everyone.
So many people have petals of mine,
And they don't even know it.
I have a wildflower for a heart,
And most days I'm okay with that,
But sometimes I wonder what it might be like
To grow in one place and not leave it.

Enough

Tell me,
Do you think it a victory,
Or an admission of defeat,
That these days,
Seeing you in my dreams is enough?

Never Falling

I close my eyes at night
And build homes inside my head.
I carve them out of memories.
I fill them up with words unsaid.
And in the ghost
Of a queen-sized bed,
I curl up in the arms
Of those I've never met.
And I feel the weight
Of the waking world
Pushing on my eyelids.
I feel the tugging at my sleeve,
I can hear reality calling.
But I don't have to leave, you see,
Because I can never hit the ground
If I was never falling.

Fever Dream

I met you last night in a fever dream,
You were lovely and I didn't want to leave.
I said, "*Where have you been? I've been waiting, dear.*"
You said, "*Darling, I've always been right here.*"
But that's not what I meant, and you knew it,
So I asked again just to be clear.
I said, "*Why can't I see you outside of my head?*"
You said, "*Darling, I've always lived in here.*"

Lake

If love is a lake
Then I'm sitting on the edge of it,
Watching others as they
Dive and float and splash,
Effortless
In the summer sun.
It looks lovely,
But it's safer here on land.
I never did learn how to swim.

Just the Wind

I thought I heard your voice today.
I could've sworn I heard my name
In the way that only you know how to say it.
But it was probably just the wind,
Howling in from outside,
Billowing the curtains with its breath.

It was probably just the wind.

I know it was just the wind.

Even so,
I'll keep my window open.

See Me

You didn't see me.
I saw myself in you,
And that's not the same thing.

Voicemail

Sometimes I wonder
Why I call at all anymore.
You never answer.
You can't come to the phone right now.
Leave a message,
Leave a message,
Leave a message.
But there's not enough space in your voicemail box.
There's not enough space in the universe.

Postcards

Do you remember when you told me
That you'd go backpacking across Europe,
And you'd send me postcards
From all the places you went?
There was so much excitement
In your glacier green eyes,
I could've bottled it.
But even then I had a feeling
That you wouldn't do those things.
Maybe you'd travel some day,
But you wouldn't send me postcards.
You never did,
And in fact, I never saw you again.
But I still think about you every now and then,
I still listen to that artist you recommended,
I still think so fondly of that excitement you held,
And I'm grateful that you said
You'd keep in touch
Instead of goodbye.

Mine

I want to enchant,
I want to haunt,
I want to be chased
But not to be caught.
I want hello
If they promise goodbye,
I want their heart,
But they can't have mine.

Horrible Things

It's a horrible thing,
But sometimes I imagine
You say horrible things.
I picture vile, vulgar, ugly words
Falling from your beautiful mouth.
You laugh at me,
You sneak and sneer,
You grow taller
As you cut me down.
I've built you up in my head, you see,
This idea of you,
This fantasy.
And like a weed,
You grow and you grow,
You trap me in vines
Covered in gold.
It's a horrible thing, I know,
But sometimes I have to imagine the thorns
To distract myself from the rose.

Dreams

The problem with me
Is that I will always love more in dreams.

A Ghost

I know that you're a ghost,
And my heart would slip right through your hands,
But I also know
That a ghost will always be solid
So long as you don't touch them.

Under a Sunset

Under a sunset,
Even a shipwreck is beautiful.
Behind rose-tinted glasses
Even disasters
Have happy-ever-afters.
If sung softly enough,
Even heartbreak doesn't sound so rough.
We can make longing so lovely,
Turn yearning and aching
Into Impressionist paintings.
So maybe, if you picture me,
Surrounded by flowers
With a deep golden sky overhead,
It won't be so hard to tell you,
That these days I'm rarely alone anymore,
But I'm lonelier than I've ever been.

Recognition

My eyes recognized something in yours:
A sadness so deep you can't see the bottom.

A Single Second

For a single second that morning,
The blanket wrapped around my body felt like an embrace,
And for a single second,
I had everything I wanted.

Monsters

I used to be scared
Of monsters reaching up the side of my bed in the dark.
I'd picture them,
These ghosts of hands reaching out,
Grasping at air,
Clawing at shadows,
Only ever seen if I dared to look,
And so I slept facing the other way.
But now that I'm older I wonder if maybe
These monsters were reaching out for a hand to hold.
Maybe they were lonely.
Maybe from now on
I'll leave my hand hanging over the side of my bed
For them to take if they need to.
Maybe I need it, too.

Tattoo

Maybe I don't want to get a tattoo.
Maybe I just want someone
To touch me tenderly, carefully,
To tell me that it's going to hurt
But hold me through the pain.

Darlings

I've killed too many darlings;
I don't have any left.
I've trimmed and cropped
And narrowed down to the bone,
But skeletons
Don't make for good company.
All I have now is myself,
Melancholic and fickle,
Solitary in nature
But lonely nonetheless.
I think I prefer the bones.
I've killed too many darlings;
I don't have any left.

Fine Line

There is a fine line
Between infatuation and love,
And I've never crossed it.
Sometimes I wonder
If I'm even capable.

What Else is New

I spent the day just thinking of you,
And it hurt,
But what else is new?

Happy

You tell me to be happy
Like it's as easy as breathing,
And maybe it is for you.
But the thing about me
That you have to understand,
Is that this sadness is built into who I am.
This sadness is stitched into me,
Embroidered on my bones,
It's tangled up like vines
On an old, abandoned house.
And you have to understand,
That to untangle that sadness
Would be to untangle myself.

Too Late

I should tell you to run,
Before your golden-hour eyes
Meet mine
And they're immortalized in gilded ink.

I should tell you to run,
Before I hear your laugh
And press the sound into prose
Like a rose between pages.

I should tell you run,
Before the warmth of your hand
Lights a fire in my heart
And I write your name with the ashes.

I should tell you to run,
But it's too late for you.

You're already poetry.

Ink Stains

I wrote your name on my hand
And the ink bled into my bones.

My skin is clean now,
But I'm not clean of you.

I don't think I want to be.

Porch Light

There is something in your eyes,
A warmth,
An open door,
A porch light left on.
And oh, I want to stand in that light.

Eyeliner

It was tenth grade.
We were in line to take our yearbook photos,
And you must have been touching up your makeup,
Because somewhere along the line I mentioned
That I'd never worn eyeliner before.
And like something out of a movie,
You grabbed me excitedly by the wrist
And whisked me away
To another room
So you could help me put some on.
I remember
You were so gentle and steady
As you applied the liner to my waterline,
Like I was something precious
Under your hands.
I think about this moment still,
The intimacy of it,
The tenderness,
Even if unintentional.
There was a magic to it
That I can't describe,
One that I'm not sure
I will ever find again.

Ribcage

I feel my ribcage tighten
Because it knows there's something inside
It's meant to be protecting.

Hide and Seek

I can never leave well enough alone,
I walk down paths I know I shouldn't go.
I take things just a little too far,
I get carried away and I know.
I'm the last one to fall asleep,
The one still playing hide and seek,
Long after they've yelled,
"Olly olly oxenfree."

Dream

If love truly is
Nothing but a dream,
Then I hope you and I
Fall asleep at the same time.

Nobody's Home

There's a door to my heart,
Wooden and old,
The doorknob rusted, worn, and cold.
You can knock all you want,
But nobody's home.

Vanishing One

I'll be the vanishing one,
The disappearing act
You didn't know had begun.
I'll leave the party early,
You won't even know I was there,
It's amazing
How easy it is in a crowd
To disappear.

Can't Heal

My heart is always hurting in a way that I can't heal.
I can't bandage a wound that I can't see.
I can't stitch together what isn't there.
I can't fill a space I don't know the shape of.

Run

I'm lying in the guest bedroom,
Staring at the blinds that cover the window,
And downstairs,
The morning starts,
Voices of those who have just woken up,
Sleepy shuffles to the kitchen,
Good morning and *how did you sleep.*
It's all so pleasant,
So quiet and normal,
But I hate it.
I don't want it.
I want to run.
I want to pack my bags and leave
To someplace far away,
Someplace where I am not a guest.
I don't want to be a guest anymore,
A spectator,
Watching as others' lives go on and on
And every night
I fall asleep in a bed that is not my own
And wake to a life that is not mine either.
The morning goes on,
So does the day.
I want to run.

Empty

I've never felt an emptiness so heavy,
A hollow so full.
I am crushed by the weight of an empty space;
I want to be whole.
I want to be whole.

Quiet and Far

"Come out, come out, wherever your are,"
"I'm going home; it's getting dark,"
"Come out, come out, wherever you are."
But I like it here
In the quiet and far.

Shattering

If ever someone were to love me,
They would have to love
The broken shards of glass
That follow me like a shadow;
I am always shattering.

How I Felt

I never told you how I felt.
I never told you that there was a spark in my chest
Every time your eyes met mine in the hallway.
How could I?
We were sixteen.
God, I was sixteen,
And I thought you were my soulmate.
Maybe you were.
I am almost thirty
But I think about you still.
Is that pathetic of me?
I was sixteen
And the idea of you consumed me.
I'm tearing up as I write this
Because god,
I was young and stupid
But god
I felt
And I felt so much.
I don't know if I've felt so much since.

Spotlights

If the spotlights shined bright enough,
Could the astronauts see us?
If I lit the street from end to end,
Would the stars think me a friend?
If I stood under a streetlight,
Would the moon give me a kiss goodnight?
How luminous must I be
For the universe to see me?
And if the universe saw me,
Would you?

Awake

I close my eyes for hours
But I never fall asleep.
I'm wide awake,
I'm wide awake,
But all I do is dream.

On the Moon

I want to be on the moon sometimes,
Because space might be dark
But it's darker down here.

Paintings

I fall in love
With paintings of people.
A portrait hanging in a gallery,
The subject in their finest,
Surrounded by what they love:
Books, flowers, a collection of art,
The whole scene
Wrapped in a gilded frame.
It's beautiful.
There is nothing in it to fear.

But a person,
A living,
Breathing,
Feeling thing,

That terrifies me.

Understand

I listen to love songs
And sing along
With a passion that suggests
I understand.

Connections

My brain is wired to make connections,
And I'm sorry if now
It connects everything to you.

There Are Stars

Night falls in my mind
As it does on Earth;
Noon fades to dusk
Fades to dark
Fades to black
And I think myself alone.

But then I look up
And there are stars.

So Bright

Sometimes I see a person so beautiful
That the thought of wanting them for myself
Feels silly.
They shine so bright
That standing in even one ray of their light
Would be enough.

Hopeless Romantic

I am a hopeless romantic
Who can do nothing but hope.
Because there's nothing more romantic than hope, is there?
There's nothing more painful, either.

Eyes Closed

I don't think I've ever been in love.
I don't think I've even come close.
Because being in love
Is looking directly into the sun,
And I've always kept my eyes closed.

Marble

I've carved you out of marble in my head,
And you're beautiful to look at,
But so cold to touch.

Art Museum

I want to go to an art museum
And get lost in a French painting.
They won't find me there.

Unreachable

You were standing in the hallway with your friend,
And I can't remember exactly
What I'd said to you,
Something mundane:
Do you have paper I could borrow?
I liked your project.
This assignment is so much work.
I can't remember,
But what I do remember
Is walking away and hearing you whisper,
"I like her,"
To the friend that was standing next to you.
I was flattered, of course,
But what struck me
Was how sad you sounded when you said it.
You said it as if you knew
That you would never be able to tell me yourself.
You said it as if you knew
That there was something about me
That was unreachable.
You were right.

I left not long after that.
But I heard you that day.
I heard you,
And I liked you too.

All I Needed

To the boy in the gray hoodie:
Thank you for asking if I was alright.
I wasn't,
But you asked,
And that was all I needed.

Winter Heart

You warm my winter heart,
You turn it into spring.
You make fields of buttercups and asters
Bloom where there was nothing.
You part the clouds above my head,
You bring the sunshine out instead,
Even if it's just for a second.
My mind is hell,
But you make it heaven.

Goodnight

When you leave,
Don't say goodbye;
Say goodnight instead.
At least then
There's the hope
That I will see you in the morning.

Leave

I could leave this place,
But I'd always find little bits of it in others,
You know?

Pressed Flowers

I've had to learn the hard way
That people aren't flowers;
I can't press them between the pages of a book
And keep them forever.

Butterflies

I have butterflies in between my bones,
They fly through my ribs and into my throat,
They've made my empty chest their home,
And it hurts, but I don't want them to go.

Even in the Stars

I held the moon in my hands
And she whispered to me,
She said,
"When the sun goes down, please speak to me.
Even in the stars, I'm lonely."

Stranger

To you,
I have become a stranger.
I don't know how it happened.
I don't know how you slipped from me so swiftly,
Like a gentle wave receding back into the ocean,
As if it wasn't crashing just moments before.

To me,
You could never be a stranger.
I knew you before I met you,
And know you still.
You're a wave that receded a long time ago,
But I'm still standing on the shore.

Forget-Me-Not

Myosotis sylvatica.
Forget-me-nots.
Baby blue flowers
Small as a fingertip.
They say,
"I will not forget you,"
But I don't need them
To remember.

Up My Sleeve

I tuck a flower behind your ear
And you wonder where it came from.
Darling, you should know by now
That I've got a whole garden up my sleeve.

Wildflower Home

Someday I will have a house made of flowers,
A wildflower home.
Overgrown and all-consuming,
No cobblestone untouched.
The flowers will be my friends;
I will take care of them,
And they will take care of me.
I will live there,
In this house of wildflowers,
Beautiful and alone.

Wish

I can't see the stars from here,
But the city lights will do.
I'll make a wish on a streetlight,
And darling,
I'll wish only for you.

Trust

I don't trust love,
I don't trust hope,
I don't trust myself,
And I don't trust you.
But I trust the petals of a rose
When they bloom.
They are beautiful and they are here,
Nothing more, nothing less.

Mon Coeur Appartient à La Lune

I do not have a lover.
My heart belongs to the moon.
She is always there
When I look up at the night sky;
A beacon of silver light.
She follows me through the trees
As we drive down the darkened highway,
Watching over me.
She holds the light of the sun
When the sun can't be in two places at once.
I am in awe of her beauty, and I envy her strength.
She has seen the world through everything
And still, she shines.

Magnetic

You were magnetic.
You must have known.
People were drawn to you like moths to a flame,
And I was no different.
The difference was that I kept my distance.

You were too bright for me.

River

You're a river.

You're a river
With water so clear
I can see the rocks at the bottom.

You're a river
And I desperately wish
I could breathe underwater.

I Am Home

I picture you in my mind,
Eyes open and soft,
Your arms around me, the most pleasant weight,
Whispering words so gentle they almost hurt
For how long I've ached for them.
I picture you,
And like a moth that's finally found the moon,
I am home.

Chanson D'amour Française

At the end of the day,
I just want someone
To lie with their head in my lap
While I run my fingers through their hair
And sing them French love songs
Until we both drift off to sleep.
Is that so much to ask?

Beautiful Things

They look like fireflies,
The city lights,
From far away.
I want to catch them and put them in a jar,
But just like the caterpillar
We tried to keep when we were eight,
We have to let some beautiful things go.

August

Eleven years ago, I said
That one of these August days,
I'd be brave.

I will admit to you now
That I was never brave.
Not in the way that I wanted to be.

I'm sorry.
I'm sorry to you
But mostly I'm sorry
To my eighteen-year-old self,
Wandering around the party after graduation,
Hoping that there was a sliver of a chance,
But still too scared to take it.

I wasn't brave then,
But I'm trying to be now.
For her.

Maybe

Maybe I believed in magic.
Maybe I believed in you.

Always

I want to be in a field of flowers,
Always,
Always,
Always.

Quietly Left

I wanted to kiss you,
But I was too scared to even talk to you.
So I did what I do best:
I quietly left.

A Place

I have a feeling there is a place
Where the fleeting and intangible
Become solid.
I have a feeling that place
Is in your hand.

6pm

It's 6pm,
I'm lying in bed,
My cat is sleeping at my feet.
There is still daylight left in the sky.
The house is mostly quiet,
And I am in pain.
My heart hurts as I write this.
There is a feeling at the back of my throat,
The feeling one gets before they cry,
And it is sitting there like a stone.
My heart is a hand reaching out,
Always, always ,always,
And always it is empty.
I ache for the day that a hand reaches back
And holds on.
I ache to feel full.
I hope I can one day come back to this poem
And know that these feelings are in the past,
But for now,
It's 6:08pm,
I'm lying in bed,
My cat has jumped off.
There is still daylight left in the sky.
The house is mostly quiet.

Carousel

My mind is a carousel,
Lovely to look at
But not to be on.
It spins and it spins and it spins,
Yet always
It stays in one place.

Insomnia

I say that I have trouble sleeping,
That every night I toss and turn
In fitful stops and starts.
But the truth is that I fell asleep a long time ago,
And I've been waiting for someone to wake me up ever since.

Anything Else

Sometimes I wonder if being lonely and wanting
Is the state I was always meant to be in,
That if I were anything else,
I wouldn't recognize myself.

The Cruelest Thing

The cruelest thing about fantasy
Is the glimmer of hope it contains.

My Heart Wants

My heart cries out
Over and over,
And I don't know how to soothe it.
I can't give it what it wants.
Because my heart wants a heart
That has the same scars.
My heart wants a mirror
Held up to itself.

Hidden

There is a side of me
That I keep deeply hidden.
It's full to the brim with lines of poetry
That lay my heart out bare,
With songs that make me cry
Every time I hear them,
With thoughts too dark to share
In such bright rooms.

I am filled with a deep, aching romanticism
That haunts me so beautifully
I can't bear to be rid of it.
It's hidden in dark corners of book shelves,
In the petals of dried roses,
Tucked away in yellowed pages
Among words that haven't seen the light of day
For decades.

And this side of me,
I want so much to share it,
But it's as fragile as the dried rose it's hidden in
And all I'm ever doing
Is looking for a pair of hands
Gentle enough to hold it.

Full of Roses

My heart is full of roses,
And they're beautiful, of course,
Blooming brilliant, vibrant,
Vivid reds.
But a heart full of roses
Is also a heart full of thorns.

If Asked

If asked why I live so much in dreams,
I might say that it's because
I love the endless possibilities that they hold.
But I think, underneath it all,
My true answer would be
That I'm scared.
I'm scared of what's real.
If I dropped a photograph of a vase,
Nothing would happen,
But if I dropped the vase itself
It would break.
Do you see?
I'm afraid to be broken,
And I'm afraid to be the one
Who does the breaking.

Someone is Home

Night has long since fallen,
The streets have all gone dark,
And I fear that finally,
I am truly all alone.
But there's a house at the end of the steet
With a light on in the window;

Someone is home.

Crushed Velvet

I long for something more,
More of what, I don't know.
I don't know if I ever will.
So in the meantime I will stay here,
Looking to the moon for answers,
Trying to find meaning
In the crushed velvet beneath my fingertips,
Planting flowers in the hopes
That they will bloom when I can't.
I will stay here and love
The warm glow of the lamp on my desk
As if it were the sun.

Quietly

I have always been quiet,
But I don't think
I could ever
Love someone quietly.

Secret

I will let you in on a secret.
The darling that I speak of in my poems
Does not exist.
'Darling' is a placeholder
For a love that I can only hope
To have someday.
'Darling' is an empty house
Waiting to be lived in.

Back Together

I can still feel the rush in my chest
From your fingertips on my face.
You held me so gently,
Like a porcelain doll
You were afraid to break.
But you didn't break me that day;
I think you put me back together.

Bit of Spring

There is something so deeply romantic
About the act of pressing flowers
And sending them in a letter.
It says *"Here is a bit of spring,*
Here is something beautiful I kept for you,
Here is a piece of where I've been."

Always Flowers

I like to remember
That even when I'm lonely,
There are still flowers.

There are always flowers.

ABOUT THE AUTHOR

Ash Elizabeth is an artist from New Jersey. Her favorite mediums include drawing, painting, and photography. Outside of art, she enjoys playing music, watching movies, and cuddling with her cat, Junebug.

Instagram: ashelizabethart
Blog: ash-elizabeth-art.tumblr.com

Printed in Poland
by Amazon Fulfillment
Poland Sp. z o.o., Wrocław
18 August 2023

8609ffd1-8111-4c5f-bf0a-9b5d273d30a0R01